Where Everything Fits Beautifully

Visit www.booksurge.com to order additional copies.

For Stormi Maya Jellison - the secret to my joy

For Keno Kendal Bradshaw - The beginning that never ends

Where is the summer that lasts forever,
The night as soft as antelope eyes?

Rita Dove-
The Snow King
Selected Poems

Lily – portrait of a secret self

My nephew
Has always
Called my mother-
His grandmother
Lily

This is not her name – my grandmother - Julia
Named her
Zuline
But she has never used this name
And will never claim it

She
Has said
Her name has been legally changed
But we, her daughters
Know this is not true

Zuline screams in black ink
From our collective birth records
Declaring us
To be the anchors
For this woman who
Has never stayed in one place without mourning
Some invisible
Unnamed loss

Often I wonder
Is there a secret self
That possesses her
That the rest of her can't see

Can my nephew sense
That essentially
His grandmother (Our mother) is
A gentle creature

Such a departure from
Who I know her to be and really
Who she has striven to be

Does this person he has dared to name
Know of us
And does she long to emerge
Become real
Forcing her captor to recede
And become
A mere apparition
Longing to embrace
Daughters that have
Fluttered in her womb
Only to be released
Dazzling butterflies

Entrapped in
A cocoon of uncertainty

How shall I feed them?
Where will they sleep?
And what of me?

Lily,
Lily,
Lily,

Sometimes
My nephew
Strokes her face
With his tiny brown
Hand as he falls to sleep

He calls her name
Like a penny is dropped into a
Wishing well

He calls
And waits

She never comes

Nine months and beyond

Underneath a moon as pale as bleached bones
She and I sit
A chasm of misunderstanding between us
The absence of all else has left us with the
Bare inevitability of who we are and what
We've become

I am her child
Yet in the comfortable anonymity provided by evening
I question the sincerity of her womb

Fate dictates she is the other side of me
In the midst of living we have lost one another
And the struggle to regain what has perished
Seems endless

Time is not kind to the pursuit of regret

Fused to our existence is an abandoned
Revolution
But
Underneath a moon as pale as bleached bones
We remain
Companioned in silence
Anchored in distance
Two halves
Of
A mythical whole

My Daughter at 10 years

Diaphanous
She
Blooms endlessly
A
Casablanca Lilly
In
Winter

My Daughter at 20 years

Fearless.
This courage of her frightens me.
I should have named this young lioness Athena,
goddess of War and Wisdom
But how was I to then, barely 20 myself, that the pink
infant
Curled in my brown arm
Would grow to be a
Warrior?

The Gathering Song

My mother's face has over time
Revealed what it never has before

There hidden in the curve of her smile
Is the story of her struggle and the secret of her joy –

There is also
The history of her mother's journey
Which of course was passed along for women
Who carried this song deeper than the subtle lines
Burrowed in otherwise flawless brown skins

You see I inherited this song and perhaps it has no
Place in my timid mouth – it seems probable there is
No refuge in my fearful soul and this leaves me at a
Loss on where to begin

You would laugh until your skin shook loose
When you learn how I first tried to tell this story
It was repossessed even before the words could form on
my tongue
I found I was forced to run after them
Dashing madly after what was promised as mine
Hair and face wild
Words fell from my mouth like broken teeth and landed
At my clumsy feet

In spite of myself I am in some part the continuation
Of those who came before me
I treasure their inherited memory – attempt to bring
Honor to what they have left me

I have felt the hollow ache of an empty womb
That yearns for the return of a lost child
The tears of an embittered bride have crossed my lips
and seared
My heart
Into my grandmother's flesh I have moved and gathered
her songs

Songs of freedom
Songs of praise – my voice is weak – unprepared to
trace the map
My mother's face has begun to reveal
But even in my ignorance
I recognize the voices of my mothers
I have determined to do them justice
To those who have been silenced
And to whom I owe my very breath
I sing aloud

Dead child to mother

Mother
Does your womb
Remember my presence
Has some part of my soul
Been left on the inside of you
At anytime
Do you long for me
As I have
For you
Is there a struggle
To recapture the butterfly
That once emerged
From the
Warmth of you-
The most intimate cocoon

Mother do you see me in your face
Is your heart stained with the
Tears I cry
Does my pain splinter
Your soul
Mother do you regret releasing me
And this silence between us
Does it leave you breathless
As it does me?

In cool evening do you hear me
Whisper your name to the trees
My secret given
To the earth

Mother
What in god's name
Have you done
With the
Memory
Of me?

Revolution

In the poetic tradition
I am recalcitrant
A body possessed of words
Seeking rebirth
Balancing rage
Against the subversively eloquent
Continually seeking to make a home for
The dialectic
Enlisting passion as a weapon of mass reconstruction

I am wind - I am air – I am legitimate
I am bastard
I am loved; I am hated, often debated
I was once held gingerly in the mouths
Of fearful queens
And spoken aloud by dubious kings
Spat at the feet of the ignorant
And given in blessings
By sons of God

Mother, whore, conformist, rebel
I am Angela Davis
Tall, tan
Waving a fist against an undulating wave of injustice

I am justified
Denied
Canonized,
Disgraced,
Dethroned,
Mystified,

I am Whitman, Giovanni and De'Castro

I am prodigal daughter
And blasphemous son

I belong to no one
And yet am possessed by many

I am,
I am,
I am,

Consumed by words
Awaiting rebirth
Gathered in me for lyrical resurrection

I am a tomb
Holding the memories
Of so many lost memories

I stand atop Baldwin's Mountain
I am Wright's Native daughter
I drink from Langston's Euphrates

I am endless in my knowing
As well as infinite in my ignorance

In poetic
Tradition
I am recalcitrant

Before, After and Again

Our hurt is collective
Gathered carelessly
Simply by living and breathing
The hypocrisies of one another

I have become a secret language
Spoken to intimate strangers
In seductive tongues
Often lost in translation
Even to those most fluent in the language
Of me

And are we not constant
Foreigners
Invading the lands and lives of those
We encounter
Plundering traditions
And pillaging familial structures

Did you notice
The breath you exhale
Is the one I inhale
It amazes me how we
Unconsciously,
Carelessly
Live off of one another
Even I refuse to speak
What I know-
Aggressively acknowledge
The need that draws me
To stay
Connected to random
Lives that serve as necessary life support

In one breathe
I take in your life, death, and rebirth
In one breathe
You release me
A reckless emergence
Tossed into abandoned space

It is ridiculous how I return to you
It is outrageous how you allow me to
Reenter you
Again, again and again

Poetic Biography

I am a forgotten Poet's Child
A lost musician's seed
And sometimes in defiance of my
Inheritance
I don't know what to write
Find myself
Struggling to
Bring pen to paper
Without bits of me
Spilling painfully to the page
My second skin shedding
Revealing
Beautiful me
Ugly me
Lost me
Whose resurrection is this anyway?

Damn,
If I don't
Find the woman in the mirror is
Radically
Changed
Somehow rearranged

I am not much more
Than I write
Nor am I less
Still I exist somewhere beyond the lines of
A page
Or at least I believe this to be the case
And so I write
Hoping to catch a glimpse of something or
Or someone else
And often I am praying
For miracles
Believing in radical transformations knowing
That who I am today
I may not be tomorrow
And so once again

I write
Trying to capture bits of myself
For myself

A subversive scheme to record
My independence

Here I am sometimes hot
Never running cold
A forgotten poet's chosen one

Struggling with words
Always these jewels gathered in my throat
Desperate for release
Threatening always to take away
The breathe of the one that
Bears them
 threatening always
To reveal me as the seed
As a lost musician
Unable and even so, unwilling to be born
Again

Human

There is beauty in
Simply
Being

Human

Miracles emerge
From hidden spaces
Left undiscovered
Within
You

Uncharted happiness
Awaits your
Entrance

And yet
You
Retreat
A warrior
Worn thin
By the simple beauty of
Being
Beautifully,
Tragically-

Human...

Mista

You are the reincarnation
Of what I thought I left
Behind
And Lord,
Mista
What do I owe?
And what more could I give
When you have
Already
Reached your hands beneath
My skin
Pulled from my bones
What ain't mine
Took strength I had on loan

See Mista-
This sista
Can't give no more and would not know
Where to find
Me
This pain runs through me on an electric current
And you come like greedy
Ocean to my
Weakened
Shores

The me my momma
Originally made
Has been left with
Another
Mista
Who took
More than I had
Put me further in
Debt

Left me wonders and words
That spill-
My blood

Overflowing across unanswered telephone lines

See Mista
I can't offer you
A reflection
Only introspection
This woman is so tired
Can't expend the energy

Struggling for approval requires
I can only you give you the abbreviated me
If even she can be found

So perhaps Mista
You should move past
This
Missus
Cause though
Blessed
I may be
First I got to recapture
The original free
That created the
Essential
Me

These brothers who live unscripted lives

Excite me
Those men who fly by the seat
Of their baggy pants
Exposing ass cracks for days
Mesmerize me

These brothers are demonized **super hero-super freaks**
They ain't got no damn plan and
Have no idea
Where the next
Day will take them
Instead these
Men/boys
Gather what is right there in front of them
And only believe what they can hold in their hands
To them
Real is obvious
It is tangible - You can pull at it with your teeth or fill your belly with its solidness
What is real is never in question
The only thing to be questioned is the motherfucker that ain't real

I am beautiful to these men
Cause I am
Right here
Larger than life
Falling into their schemes
And believing in their magic
They love my fullness
Softness
Womaness
And they tell me in voices hoarse with
Hustle
How a woman like me is so hard to find
But even harder to keep

My father was one of these men
Always inventing new shit
And dismantling useless shit
Not staying long enough
Or perhaps overstaying his welcome in unfortunate
places
These men
Are in my blood
Damning me with their persistence
And pretty smiles
They even walk pretty and
They sure do smell pretty

And lie lovely

I love these brothers who live unscripted lives
I love them easy, willingly – persistently.
I love them like they are my first drink of water
or my last breath of air
I love these brothers who fly by the seat of their pants
Showing ass crack for days
Leaving mesmerized
Women like
Me
Trembling in
Their wake
with nothing more than memories of their superhero
superfreakness
to sustain
us

Salt Water

Out of my mouth
Into your trembling hands fell my
Confession
Every lie I've told
Was stripped to its pale, glimmering bone
And I stood still as the raw truths I'd hidden
Swirled about me, grabbed hold and dragged me
Helplessly along
Captured I came away without
Resistance like the soft flesh of a dying flower
I caught a glimpse of you
Standing along an impossibly distant
Shore
Refusing to be an anchor
There you stood with only fear
As your shelter
Perhaps you called out to me
But I did not hear
So busy was I struggling
Against sudden flight
I believe you remained
Rooted
As if you'd
Sprung from the very ground
On which you
Stood
Drawn along the precipice
Of complete resignation
I give absolute surrender
To the waves that crash at my
Feet
Take like a fish
To the salt water that engulfs
Me

An Infant Africa

I was once a wilderness
My self-preservation existed in what
I had yet to discover

I am now a dark continent
At the shore of me
Men greedily sweep away
The landscape,
Leave behind
What they
Cannot put
To use
Tear down my forests,
Construct their cities
Buildings
That block
The sunlight
Cover my lands
Destroy my wilderness
Leave me naked
Somehow,
Shamed
My dignity
They wrap about
Their shoulders
Dress their tables
And feed their young
The memory of me
Lingers on their
Pink tongues
Runs warm in their bones
I am a dark continent
And I was once
A beautiful wilderness

Undiscovered...

Untitled # 1

This is for the unborn I scattered carelessly
The sons and daughters
I recklessly pulled from me
I wonder if you were
To be gathered
Whole
Would you fold
Yourselves
Once again into me
And what choice would I make
When faced with your resurrection-
And of your
Fathers
Are they as culpable as I?
Do I alone bear the sins
Of your improbable deaths and subsequent
Rebirths,
Do I owe you life and if so
Should I repay my debt
With my life
Lost children of mine
In your heaven
Do you call me
Mother
Or have you captured the fractured spirit of another
Dear ones,
Do you long
For childhood
As I now long for your broken bodies to be mended?
Dear ones, have you released me even as I seek to
grasp you?
Or have you forgotten me;
The one who scattered your lives
Carelessly to
The
Wind.

The Memory of Beautiful

This is the prayer of the lonely sister
Long after the babies have fallen to sleep
In the hours
Before the sun rises
And she is left with
The remains of some man
Who has once again taken too much
This sister prays that
The wants of others will not drown her
She prays today
If only for a moment
She will catch a glimpse of herself and feel
Beautiful
For once
Her smile will be enough for someone
Perhaps
She will be seen
Not look through-
No more a mere distraction-just for today
Today she will be loved

Beautifully

She won't be
The caregiver
Bill payer
Hustler
Pimp
she has become-
Somehow she
Has evolved effortlessly into a shadow
Of the self her Momma originally created
She remembers beautiful-
Can easily recall
Some abstract independence
She remembers,
And now her prayer
Before the babies awake tugging innocently at the worn
fabric of her

And the solitude of the night
Dissipates-
Is to have some part of that lost
Woman
Return.

The Secret Language of Women

I know the secret language of women
And when I speak
Perhaps you will hear
The voices of those who sang
Majestically before me
Mary's moans
And Martha's weeping
Billie Holiday
Keeping
Royal court
And if you look closely
You will see the ghosts of strange fruit
Once borne on Southern trees
Perhaps the smell of death
Will lull you to cruel sleep
As it has me
Catch a glimpse of Sara Vaughn's tomorrow
And at last be blessed by Etta's joy
I speak the secret language of women
I sing with the voices of my foremothers
I am the daughter
They cried to, begged, fought and shed layers of
Dignity for-
Mothers
Do you recognize me and when I speak or sing
Does what I say do you justice
I am this Northern girl
Who ran to the bosom of the South
The womb of my mothers,
The prison of my fathers
And still the ground screams
With blood
Violent hieroglyphics
Etched on restless souls…

Dedicated to Julia Elizabeth Postles

Learning to sing like Lady Day

In a brave imitation of you
I tucked a brilliant flower
behind my ear
painted my lips
fire engine red
and wore my sorrow about my shoulders
as if it were a mink coat
imagining I was you reborn
I straightened my back, straining each muscle with
dignity
worn thin by an ungrateful world
I leaned my head back and opened my mouth
and
let my loves, losses, and triumphs
tumble forward...
in each note
I bore some truth that revealed more of you
I sing as you would
to the lovers gone too soon
sweeping bits of me away with each hasty
departure
I am shore to their greedy oceans
to the unborn
not yet mine
I sing as only a woman full of longing can
I mourn the first heartache
I rejoice the first victory
I am mother
unfulfilled
I am lover
Unrepentant, rebellious in my loneliness
You see mother,
I too, have seen the strange fruit
born by Southern trees
singing from the center of self,
I walk along the edges of you-
a buffer
to guard your war weary bones

from the burdens of others
against this storm, mother
I remain steadfast
A brilliant flower tucked behind my ear,
An unfinished song in my mouth

Circumcisions

Black girls
are having their sexuality
sacrificed
one
clitoris
at
a
time

Their lips
are being sewn shut with coarse string in crude huts
by blind women who fail to see their
role in silencing a generation of mothers
before their
womanhood can begin to bud
and somehow
I am carrying the lost lives
of these sisters
afraid to speak their names
aloud
for fear
I may loose these fragile beings
to some strong wind
that will carry off the secret of their underground selves
that will once again steal them
rape them
make then unwilling
concubines in an unnamed government
struggle
that fuels
some blasphemous dream
and what then?

No body knows
what then?
Leads to
I am hesitant to join the legions of
blind mothers
who fail to see
the destruction of their

daughters

I am in the name of my daughter will be the
Warrior,
bitch –
another
"Who the fuck does she think she is?"

I am
fighting so she will not
be another number
another body
another woman
given
to being the silent
power

In the name of my daughter
I will not
be a blind mother
cutting her parts
to pieces
scattering them to unknown places

It is the least I can do

Sincerity

You question-
ask with menace
laced with graciousness
If I am
satisfied with who I have become
you want
to know do I treasure
everything I am

You want to know
the source
of my poetry
what makes the words
flow
like water and
fall like jewels
from my mouth
landing at the feet
of folks
starved for more of what I have created

I can't explain my own
joy except
to know
inherently I have earned
this blessing of light after a lifetime
in shadow

See dearest one,
I believe you
ask because
your winter
is endless and you
envy my
eternal
spring

Skeleton

The bones held in this
black skin
are the same that have held strong
when lord knows they should have fallen
weak
a
longtime ago
these bones have carried the burgeoning weight of
children
now grown and gone
to distant lives
but still managing to pull some of me
from the marrow that remains,
now these bones rattle restlessly in the tired
skin
that bears them-
if these bones should just fall to the red earth
and shed the fleshy shelter that has grown about them
would they then long for the familiar comfort of being?
or would they rejoice
in the random freedom of being scattered
would they somehow gather themselves to be rejoined?
or would they remain disjointed
satisfied
with stealing independence
and basking in unheralded resurrection
while defining wholeness in the connected lives of
others?

War

I ain't going to study war no more
I am so tired of shaking my skin loose
only to begin again, again and again

I ain't going to study war no more
Using my body as battleground
pilfering joy
from some momma's selfish little boy
reaching through the ghost of some other
taking back me
piece by piece
bit by bit
and what I take is the least of my being
the best is held hostage
under brutal sky and wounded stars
buried in the marrow of another

The joy that runs
through me threatens to clot
causing me to have a stroke
or heart attack
fall dead
right in the middle of this war
still find I this elusive treasure
runs across the pink tongue of his
too greedy mouth
slips down his chin
tempting me to put my mouth
where it don't belong
cause I am longing to taste
what it is
he can't
stop consuming

I ain't going to study war no more
and even as I say this
I have yet to lay down my weapons

these breasts that ache
and unreasonably long for his touch

The crossroad at the center of me
composed of the most malleable metal
inviting him to enter
endlessly
so much so
time moves to catch us
comes waving a white flag
imploring us to slow down
as we in battle
crash hungrily into one another –
recklessly tear away the armor
of the other
greedily take what we should not
and now I am this
tiny soldier
the david
to his GOLIATH
having allowed the enemy
to cross over into and through me
I
have willing sacrificed my free
surrendered without completely giving me only to find
the war that rages is
the battle already lost…

Conversation

When I tell her all over the world
Women are suffering injustices and being exploited
continuously, I can barely tell if she is
still on the phone. She has slipped into silence and I can
only hear her breathing-
Steady
In and out
Soft puffs of air that she releases and pulls back into her
body
She finally speaks – tells me as casually as asking for a
cup of tea or even a request that I pass
The sugar
As simple as that, she speaks to me as if I am naughty
Bad girl
You say bad things, I imagine her waving her finger.
I have always thought her nails are two short, not nearly
becoming a lady – or a human for that matter.
She always tells me not to get started, don't start on that
race thing or the feminist whatever or another.
And now I am exasperated because she always does
this, calls me and does not really want to talk.
It seems she is always drunk with sleepiness or
nonchalance or ignorance. It is intoxicating, really, to be
this oblivious or indifferent or just so insulated, so warm
in nothingness that you begin to doze.
I am naughty
Because all the time I am thinking
Thinking too much and this is not nearly becoming for a
lady, but it may be all right for a human.
I am aware of her breathing again
Soft pulls
In
And out
There are women like us, with bodies like us,
disconnected from us, I protest.
In and Out.
Hello?
She has fallen silent. So quiet I imagine I can hear the
soft thump of her heart across the telephone line.

Look, that's their religion or whatever. Don't you get
started – I told you, it's always something or another with
you.
My daughter runs into the room, interrupting as usual
with this or that. I am always
Drawn into her pleas
Soft pulls
That are endless
I 'll call you tomorrow

In

For a moment I have forgotten she was there, listening
to me, inventorying my daughter's behests for attention –
she, my daughter, is a good girl, but Jesus – she flutters
like a butterfly-
And
Out

It is an exit not nearly becoming a lady, or a human for
that matter.

Distance

(A poem found in a notebook I carried from North
Carolina to Massachusetts – it has followed me like a
lost dog, only to move into the pages of this book –
home at last.)

When women run
They pound pavements with feet
And bodies aligned towards rumors of freedom
And away from homes
Holding secrets resembling
Unwanted
Pregnancies

Often unsure
Of the place
Meant to sustain them
Hold them,
Guard them,
They (these running women) measure
Their weight
Against formidable
Storms
Without knowing
Exactly
The definition
Of respite
Or where it is housed

When women
Run
The running
Out distances
Their
Sacred
Selves
Leaves
Them pining
For the
Holiness

Of simply being
Still

The First Kiss

In morning
The grass is bent
With crystal dew
Greedily pulling it forward to meet the moistened ground,
eagerly awaiting
the first silken kiss.

White Girl – For Heather

She is a Southern White girl
Possessed of a plural conscience and a weakened
allegiance
To her beginnings
So she believes she pays tribute to me
Because she loves black men and has had caramel
colored babies
By a nameless few
She would not care to mention save for the fact she feels
this in some way
Allows her into a society of women who tolerate her
presence
But
Secretly abhor her intrusion

Of all the things she could worry for her children
She's just glad they were "blessed" with good hair and
as much as she loves
Black
At least when it is wrapped around the body of a man
She 's just glad her kids aren't too dark
Because that is a reality she never prepared herself for
And being black has always been easier when it is not
entirely permanent

She don't give a damn about cancer or wrinkling too
soon – so she tans everyday
In her mind there are no shades of gray
And the definition of white has always escaped her
But black
Why, that is simple as mom's apple pie
How deep does that go?
To emulate is far easier than any academic investigation
Would allow
As far as she can see fucking a scholar was never on
the agenda and
That would never rile the family despising her choices
Quite like bringing home some
Do-rag wearing, illiterate
Bastard son of a bitch

To disrupt daddy's dinner
And then announce that this is my man of the moment –

Fuck Cornell West
This is what matters
Crossing the line without being seen

This Southern White girl
Has dyed away the blonde, cultivates her hips likes
some grow rose bushes or a garden in
A suburb
Where we would all want to be
Cause god's children are tired of making do
With making ugly less ugly
And as much as we scrub it
This place makes us all so damn tired
And we are tired-
Tired of being wrongly emulated
And imitated
We are tired of having our backs used as bridges and
we are tired
Of having our humanity disrespected
And of our men going to women like her
And disregarding our struggle
We are their mothers, daughters, and sisters
But the obvious truths bear indelible hurts
And this is what we are left with

Nothing that really matters

And does she participate in the struggle
When she has a dual self?

A subversive reality, carrying oppressive comforts
Escaping the rest of us colored folks

She is not me
And could not
Even if she saved forever
Purchase my knowing
To her I am an indecipherable anomaly
And she has no idea
Of why any of us can continue to rise and love -

Love until we are dry from loving so much
We are not carved from rock
There hidden in the marrow of our strength is our
gentleness
We are soft as the underside of a dove's wing
Love us and see
Just witness how we care for our young – watch and you
will
See us
Black women
Though lonely like the stars in
Solitary night
Watch us
continue to rise - a force unto ourselves
see us dispense
Love,
Cautiously
Softly
Freely

This white girl
Don't know black
Because she would have to know me

And that was never
On the fucking agenda…

May 27, 2006

If I had an eraser
I would remove every
Reminder of those
Who were once here
And took too much of me
For themselves
I am speaking of those brothers
Who
Emotionally mutilated

Me

While
I smiled
Pleasantly
And feigned conformity
In the form
Of absolute servitude
This is the worst
Rape
When I am a participant in my own
Destruction
This is the most brutal
Betrayal

Contrition

It is like I am holding the knife
To my own throat
Even my blood
Screams as a witness
A crimson rose
At my lost feet
Revealing a thousand
Truths

If I could I would
Take every piece of me
Back
I would gather myself whole

Unscathed
A sword
Return to its scabbard

Repossessed – Potentially
deadly

Hera

See that sister over there with the cowry shells
Woven in her dreadlocked hair?
She has flowers tattooed on her hands and feet-
Woven around her ankles in black and red
Are roses eternally in bloom

This urban Juno is dreaming of foreign soil-
Dust, crimson as dried blood, stains the souls of her feet

Awash in sunlight
She has been seduced by the day
Oblivious to those brought to their knees before her

She secrets her joy
Could shake loose her skin and be born again if she
choose
But

There she is
With remnants her journeys entangled in her hair and
Trapped beneath her nails

Long awaited answers are yet to fall graciously from her
smile

She knows far more than she reveals
Her knowing is told in the soft
Sway of her hips
Kept sacred by wisdom
Imparted by those who came before her
Bestowed gifts
She now treasures
Has taken into herself to be reborn
Amidst the rubble of a thousand yesterdays
There lie the lovely bones of tomorrow
Awaiting resurrection
As this modern day
Hera
Remains awash in sunlight
Seduced by the day

Last Night

Last night a poet saved my life
Reached through my soul
With ancient hands
Gathered my pain and sealed it in ancient tombs
Along the Valley of the Kings
Gave me over to queens and goddesses
Nefertiti and Isis
Who in turn, snatched me from Osiris
These mothers
Soothed me with words
Gathered from the four corners of the earth
This poet
Immersed me in verse
And wet nursed me with the milk of his wisdom

Last night a poet saved my life
Built as though he could snatch a star from sky
He made love to me
And released me to me
Gave me some part of his soul
Imprinted with magical lyricism
He whispered the secrets of time into my ear
Allowed my tears to soak his dreads

Last night a poet saved my life
Words fell as jewels from his precious mouth
Left me naked with truths upon truths
Pulling me from a spiritual wreckage
He breathed life into my fractured spirit

Last night a poet saved my life

Lion of Judah   (For, Judah)

Brother,
You say you want to love me
Own me
Imprint your name on the inside of me
But I say
My soul
Is sacred and I need a man
Who can snatch stars from the sky
And place them sincerely in my trembling
Palms

Brother,
Can you brave the Sun
Walk along its surface, grasp fire
Place it within my cold heart and make me
Turn inside out to leave behind the ghosts of former
selves?

Brother, you must be magical
Composed of our forefathers spirits, warriors, kings,
Nubian Scholars
You must be descended from the Tribe of Judah –
respectful of our past
Prepared to build our future
You must come
Bearing the gifts of earth, wind and fire

If possible you will reduce the space between us to
nothing
Air will be a hindrance and we will become so entangled
in the
Other
The beginning and the end
Will be as one –
We are now Adam and Eve incarnate

I, in turn
Will be the mother, daughter, whore, and lover
You incessantly crave
Universe will be my name, and I like she was born on
the 7th day

You, as the Titans before you
Will bear me upon your shoulders
Converse with the Gods and
Whisper their secrets in my ears
Universe will be my name, you will feel
Life and death
Pass through my sacredness
You will as a tree
Grow into me
Witness life bear its precious fruit
Accept that I offer you my sky
And my heaven and deny you the rages of my hell
Brother before you seek to imprint your name on the
inside of me
Truly know the wall upon which you write

Speak

She builds a tree from bones gathered
In her garden
Takes each bare limb into her capable hands and
reanimates
The dead
Pulling secrets from the sealed earth is tedious work
Causes her to rethink resistance and replant what she
has
Gathered in more fertile land
She is now an unwilling goddess
Falling backward into otherwise
Beautifully complicated dreams that bloom
Into drastic realities
harboring the raging spirits of the forgotten dead

For Dana - the one who walks among the dead

I don't come with the vagina monologues
But rather a heart to head dialogue
I come with the purpose to lift you like botox
        Cleanse you like detox
Because you see
I have been on my knees
Begging for reciprocity
Allowing another
To weigh their sins against
        Me
 And I loved one so insincere
That even his seed would not attach to me
        And now I pour water
        At the altar
Of a mutual failing
I alone loved and still mourn
The life that refused to cross over through me
And to him that refused me
The father that was not to be
I could gather him into my mouth
Only to spit him whole into his mother's insincere womb
        Allow her to suffer being a living tomb

Her son is the thief that stole my innocence
        The liar who
Disrespected my blessedness

 I come for your hearts
As I have lost mine
I come for your souls
For mine I traded
Left at the door
Of the one who refused me
Kindness,
        humanity
The simple gift of reciprocity

Winter

On the crumbling corner of Roanoke and Boston
They stand together

Yet separate

With ashen faces
That have somehow lost definition and blend
Seamlessly into one another
Their backs are turned away from the wind that
Curls itself around their thin bodies
Stealthily burrows its cruel breath
Beneath their tough skins
And seeps into fragile bones

In summer
The stale scent of not having clings to these
Children
Becomes entangled in their wild hair
And glistens like freshly fallen dew
On their
        Black skins

In Finite

We are these poets

Infinitely lost

Seeking tribes
To fold ourselves into

Words fall to us

Lyrical

Manna

We
Manically
Consume
And
Regurgitate
As
Psalms
To an insatiable,
Invisible god

Wellspring

Before the day can barely begin to bud
I am already wishing silently, ruefully for its dissolution

The woman in the mirror
Gives obvious
Testimony to what lies ahead

Around me the house moves into life
Begins to take hold of the day
Its inhabitants are dependant
On my resourcefulness

Despite my resistance I am drawn into the process of
living and made whole
By the mundane acts that provide vital sustenance

There is no redemption in surrender

I move with singular purpose – reminiscing briefly on
what
May have been before every piece of me was portioned
off for the benefit of others

Contrary to my desperate lack of ownership
Joy manages to reside in my bones

I have evolved to become eternal
I am life giving in the many roles I am destined to play
There is no end to this metamorphous
Despite the obvious testimony
The woman in the mirror provides

Home

Here I am driving along
Some anonymous road
A blur of green daring to reach towards a blue strip of
sky

Yawning black before me the road curves endlessly,
seems to wrap itself
Around my journey
Pushing me gently forward

My daughter for once
Not restless
Sleeps soundly
Her body curled comfortably
Around the jazz
That plays softly
Soothing us both
As we head towards a place of our
Own

Cave

The hollow mouth of earth
Is sheltered unto itself
Life – graciously foreign
Evolves into a bastard truth
While the depths of undiscovered territory is left
To rampant
Wilderness
light, helpless in its endless evolution
Gives casual surrender
To the carnivorous darkness that
Greedily swallows it

Freestyle (For those Supreme Sisters - you know who you be)

She is this sister continuously raging
engaging in random revolutions
requiring radical evolutions
and often she finds
the problems damn the solutions
making her want to walk in the other direction
take every thing she has stored and place it gently on
the back of another
because even a minute of rest would amount to
something
more than this constant pulling -
making do is making real from nothing - like magic
all of a sudden, sister is a ghetto Houdini - pulling tricks
to make shit happen
You see
sister is blindly
gathering strength from hidden places
these are places
she had no idea existed,
so deep in her they hide
these caverns of power
often she awakes
with this fear caught in her throat,
some concern or worry over
another slice of bullshit she unintentionally had for
dinner and now it has found it's way to her again in the
middle of the night
like some kind of societal heartburn and she settles the
burn with
an antacid composed of a retarded kind of hope - the
kind of hope that is missing a chromosome and
dissipates before it can fully form . It would take a team
of surgeons to separate this deformed emotion from the
one who birthed it -
Because sister still carried it - nurtured it - kept it close -
hoping it would live and every time this hope dies, she
longs to carry it again - a brutal pregnancy that makes

you understand why some animals chose to devour their
young
So this is what she deals with
In the evening when her daughter is curled against her
Sister can only manage to pray struggling and not
having is not contagious - she wills fiercely it will not
burrow itself beneath the skin of her child and
leave her rummaging for homemade panaceas that
spark random revolutions and
radical evolutions that manage to create problems
continually damning the solutions

222 Words

Most times I am struggling
Searching
Bending –
Stealing words
That belong in another's mouth
Just so I can express myself
Correctly –
Eloquently
But often I find what I say
Falls short of what I feel and there is no hunger
Like the ache of a lost thought
Or unexpressed emotion

And silence is a blessing often overlooked -
Misunderstood
If I could remain hushed
I probably would discover what it is I think I lost
And perhaps the world would open up to me
Eager to fill the space left by my rambling words
And my grandmother often
Said
I speak just to hear myself talk
And half of what I say don't amount to much
Of nothing
But still I talk – thinking what I am saying is saving
someone
From forgetting I am there
And now I think if they forget
Than this is my blessing
Because if I am so easily lost
I was never there
And speaking does not represent all of me
Just the me that needs to be heard
And often I measure the weight of a picture against what
I am saying and have come to
The conclusion that what I am saying is my portrait
Take time to read me
See me

222 words are all it took to compose this picture anyway.

A Lyrical Fairy tale (Told in the first person)

I am to words
What air be to lungs
Uplifting, continually gifting ears
With a poetic, prophetic
Hustle and flow
A lyrical traveler, the poetic
Gretel
To a yet be found wordsmith Hansel
And once found – me and he
drop verse like breadcrumbs
Leaving our footprints on snowdrift sentences
While navigating
Weather worn words
To find our way
Home

Untitled #48

Forgiveness

Is me unfolding
Endlessly

Healing
Is you
Not bruising
The softness that is exposed

When
You
Re-enter

Plan B (For the US i know we to be)

On a sunny, party cloudy
Saturday afternoon
I asked
you
800 miles or more away -where the sun managed
a radical departure from stubborn clouds determined to
steal it's brightness;
on this afternoon I ventured a question
concerning
Plan B just in Case your plan A
emerged stillborn
I am only asking cause my dreams have become so
entangled in yours
I am already putting furniture in our house and baking
organic, whole wheat bread to the sounds of joyful
children declaring us to be real -
by my count there are two girls and two boys
who collectively
claim us as some part of them -

Plan B
is mending
concealing -
righting and redoing the wrongs before
the WE
that defines US
came into existence
Plan B is you loving me and the seeds
that spring from us, we are now fertile lands
merged to form a nation of our own
This is me
with arms outstretched
gathering dreams like flowers and churning them into
beautiful realness
You asked me of my plan B
and I could only stand in the shade
of a passing cloud - finding the sun had surrendered, at
least momentarily - to give it's brilliance over to the

endless sky who in turn was eager to temporarily gobble
it's fire with a carnivorous blue mouth...
And for the briefest of moments, I found silence filled the
distance between us better than words
You see, I have no Plan B - there is no contingency plan,
no shelter for disaster and damn, I should know better –
but this time, for the last time, I am going to allow this to
grow wildly, undisciplined - I have no room for more
stillborn dreams, too many of these I have buried with
grief that threatened to eviscerate me, so malevolent it
was
These dead dreams suffered unceremonious deaths that
marked the loss of some part of me I am now better off
without, some part of me that lies in an unmarked grave
-
This reanimated me would rather bask in the
glow of your Plan B, now my Plan A
I would rather gather these dreams that shake free of
you only to land in my outstretched arms
eager to be churned into beautiful realness...

The Last Breath

Gathering in the hollow
Of my chest
It curls itself coolly around organs
Determined to keep me alive
It fills the soft pink flesh of my lungs only to
Settle briefly in the hollow of my belly
Down
        Down
To my toes
It unfurls
And snakes its way back to the
        Center
Of me
Blossoms invisibly in my mouth
Leaving silken petals on my tongue
When I speak I litter the air
With what has been inside of me
Even as I am silent
There I am being captured and released by
Foreign bodies
        Thrown
Willy-nilly
Into the atmosphere
I tumble carelessly from mouth to mouth
A body in constant
motion

An Incantation for the Mad

I am swallowing dignity and survival
And shitting
An all too familiar
Promiscuous rage
I am coming up for water
And drowning in air
Lately holding hands with God
Feels like waking up with the Devil
The Universe has held this unreasonable rage and me
Once before
Only to release and rebirth me
Here I stand
Cutting my skin to release
Angels trapped darkly humming hymns and sacraments
I suppose these are supernatural blessings for the
blasphemous
I am
Inhaling demons
And exhaling multiple sins
Intimacies have become sandpaper on tissue paper skin
I remember nothing before this anger –
There are times I hunger for the brutal comfort of
confrontation –
If disarticulated and reassembled I can only imagine
these emotions would find themselves
Radically relocated
I would piss happiness and digest bitterness – and
continue to shit a
Rage that has a way of replicating itself endlessly
In this I am immortal
In this I am the mirror image of my father
The God of all necessary things

More Like her

Because she moved from her parents home to a pristine
Palace in Jamaica Plain
I am invisible to her or perhaps too visible – my
presence screams like a splash of angry red paint
against cream-colored walls
I am an unfortunate Jackson Pollack in a room of
redundant Monet's.
She cannot seem to wrap her head
Around my existence
And every breath I take
Further confounds her
Should I not be more ladylike
Or at least more like her
Name my children
Julia,
Elizabeth
Or Kelsey
Should I not on weekends
Bake,
Clean,
Fuck my husband until he forgets the names of others
Perhaps more skilled
Than I
Women who loom like poltergeists in his distant past
And often these harpies disrupt his dreams – beckoning
him to their open mouths with endless throats and
promises of blossoming fully on their welcome mat
tongues
She digests the memories of these women
As easily as she regurgitates the reality of me – I believe
I push the boundaries of reality too far for once such as
her
I loom to close too what could have been her if not for
the diligence of her immigrant parents determined to see
their daughter shake free their small island
accoutrements – and the closest she will now come to
home is a Mango Marguerita on Newbury Street
I, the thrift shop fashionista am I singular, blaring,
unabashed offense

Would it not be better if I simply lived more complicated
– gave more credence to inane conformity
Then she would not be forced to deny her judgment –
rather she could bask in it – a lioness warmed by a
Specific sun, designed to her liking
If I only I could I would
Be more like her
I could enter her life – a medium of sorts
And channel her perfection through my unabashed
imperfections – gather her pleasantries and masquerade
them as mine
And in turn I would be haunted by her
The harpie who disrupts my husbands dreams,
beckoning with her open mouth – endless throat –the
one that threatens pleasure by swallowing him whole
The poltergeist she once dared not be

Him

I keep the secret of him tucked beneath my tongue or
At least that is where I store
The goodness of him
The part that I need to remember when I so often, too
often, loose track of
Who he is
In this warm, forbidden darkness I release him
Slowly
Only to devour him
And then
refill my eager, insatiable mouth
Again and again with who he is
The aftertaste
lingers sweetly
A hungry child cradled in my mouth
Grabbing ferociously for the bits of him that
Have hidden in between tooth and gum
Or the empty pocket of flesh left
From an extraction -
The spot that still throbs when touched by cold

The rest of him – the part not kept safe by the haven
provided by
The underside of my tongue is lovely with ferociousness
This part stains my body inside and out – leaves me
black and blue with random realities
revealing his all-too radical self
this part of him is caught in my wild hair
trapped beneath my nails
traces of him appear
like ghosts on the surface of me
often coloring me with variations of who he is at any
given moment
and of course – he never remains the same person
I could never pocket his free
Never grasp his wanderings
I can only manage to envy his fearless roaming
In his absences
My neck screams with the roughness of his kiss

My arms plead for mercy – telling me to push him further
and harder into me
I should instead separate myself from the succubus that
is him

When he is near
I am too often
Reaching out to implant some part of me on him
And this he will not allow
Too much of a guardian of his soul is he to permit this
And I have become a guardian of him as well
Careful to tuck him neatly
In a place that only I can access
He has no idea
That he occupies
Rooms and places of my creation
And speaks when I say speak
And the words
That fall
Are what I desire to hear

He has no idea
I have somehow managed to grasp the free
He failed to guard

The realties of him
Rival the imagined possibilities I have established
Still
These
Secrets reside
Beneath my tongue
Resonating black and blue
With
Beautiful deception

Solidarity Song

This is for Vernon Dahmer
George Jackson and the Soledad Brothers
Dr. Angela Davis
Nikki Giovanni
And Sonia Sanchez

Hell, let me mention Emily Dickinson, Walt Whitman
Truman Capote
And Dr. Charles Drew

Because no one remembers the words
To Plantation Lullabies
or at least
These songs remain lodged in fearful throats
Unheard
Unimagined
Unsung

This is for those resplendent in their struggle
And magnificent in their survival

I envy you

I covet the strength you guard
With your life

Just because
No one is talking
About justice
Or injustice
And too few are making beauty from nothing
Except maybe
Those baby mommas everyone is talking about –
You know them gals
That have those beautiful, beautiful babies
But barely have love to give them –
I guess they be the words
In too many forgotten lullabies
Draping themselves

In someone else's dreams and financing undocumented
lives
on uncharitable charity

I think I should mention
The woman at the check cashing place
Her man, leaning into her like a worn tree –
This woman with dark eyes
That mark endings and no beginnings
Turned to me and said,
Sometimes I wish I were White

Well, this is for her
Because
She was tired
With her man leaning into her
And she just wished her self away
Like she was nothing
And nowhere
And right before me she was gone
Leaving too much beauty behind

Those eyes
That told of nothing
And that smile that said less
There is much to be said for silence

So this is for her
For giving up
And leaving me
With her plantation lullaby
Unheard
Unimagined
Unsung

Until now.

The secret of US

Black as day
Sweet as sin
Precious secrets hide themselves
Fitfully in the curves that define me
There in the curve of my arm
Where delicate flesh avoids brutality
But somehow still
bruises
Is the truth of you
I keep you there –
Silent and protected
Away from the mouths
Of others
Who search and covet
And here
In the space between neck and ear
Is the love
I reserved for another
The one
Who now loves me
Despite
The
Memory of us
Tucked beneath each
Breast
And captured at the meeting
Of thighs
The same limbs that once pulled you
Too close
Almost into my marrow –
I used you as a weapon
To battle myself
Into desperate submission
Only to see you wrestle free
And leave
Your footprints
In the
Line of my back
Along my buttocks

And my heart, the most secret place of all – this is where
you still reside – a beautiful boy, never turned man –
living in me as a bird does a hollow tree
Nibbling at the love that should have long since passed
and perhaps has
But there are crumbs that remain
(As with any good meal)
And you
Beautiful boy
Pick fitfully
At the secret that resides and sustains
Us
Both

Zuline's Girls

Of all the things,
My mother's daughters could have inherited from her
We
Choose in lieu of her extraordinary proclivity for cruelty
Her appetite for other people's men
This collective choice has left us
Insatiable
Often seeking to complete ourselves
In the incomplete
Or downright greedy
We give away our essential selves easily
Leaving our bodies behind
Like husks
Flattened and useless
While we transcend morality - intertwine our souls, our lives
in the tangled flow of men with women who are aware of us
And pity our solemn desperation
So they leave us
To their men
Leave us to love them with no threat of reciprocation –
this is their
Gift to their man kind
Women like us – with nothing or no one to truthfully anchor or pull us safely ashore
The traces of ourselves we purposefully leave behind declare our sorrowful needs
And these other Women, the ones who belong – whose homes we momentarily invade have mercy on us – the others who forage like animals for scraps of stability that have been
Lost to us

We take what we can

Because we – us sad orphaned girls have been mothered by the random and indifferent
Those with no knowledge of the beginnings and in-betweens that define us

Our true mother regards
Us as we
Are
Simply
Recycled, misguided revolutionaries
Loving other peoples
Men
Time and time
Again –
It is what we have chosen
In lieu of her proclivity for extraordinary cruelty

Roxy (Though I do not remember meeting you)

I think you may have left the secret of yourself
behind - intertwined in the seemingly inanimate
your joy resonates beautifully
echoing itself
in the laughter of children
and leaving you in yet to be discovered places
There in the soft blossoming of spring
you emerge -
in the fickle temperament of winter
you fitfully reside

you may have
given the memory of your grace
to the earth
so we may be witnesses
to your
eternal rebirth and continual defiance
of death

All black children are not bastards
This is what I
In anger
Declare
To a faceless
Teacher
Who can't recall my name
Though she has called me with regard to my
Daughter
Who carries the same last name as me
This for reasons known and internalized by us both
Seems to baffle her
Causes her to drop the sentence she was forming
As if it tasted as bad as it sounded
And could possibly stain her mouth with the ugliness
It belies
Oh, she says and there for a moment, is just the sound
of paper shuffling
Am I somewhere amongst scraps of paper – has she
jotted a note to herself
Perhaps a hasty reminder to contact the mother
Of an untamed child – allowed to grow wildly – no fence
posts to hold her in or stop her
From aspiring to unnamed heights
In this I have been irresponsible
I have failed to reign in the spirit that is my daughter – I
have not schooled her on limitations
Or dreams deferred
I have been notoriously negligent in stifling her freedom
I can clearly see this teacher rearranging the picture of
me formed in her head.
We have entered into fierce battle – this teacher and I
I am wondering how this woman
Who disregards my name
Can be teaching my child
Does she even know whom she teaches
Or is my child,
In her eyes
An unfortunate extension of me
I imagine, if we were to meet – she would not look me in
the eyes
Hers is a divine mission

To stop the rose before it can bloom
And she is aware, though never a true witness, to how successful she has been
These poor children
With these pitiful mothers believe her declarations of failure
Take what she, this reckless teacher, has decried and pulls the words into their marrow
There failure only metastasizes and eventually devours the life that resides fitfully
She's teaching them responsibility or as least that is the word in the teacher's lounge
The place where students and parents are forbidden
Yet they, these secretive ones, raid our homes and lives
For evidence of failure
And once a tiny speck is found
Perhaps an unmade bed or a grumbling belly
Then we/us is declared unfit
We are incorrigible
We are negligent
We are the mothers
Who rise to struggle and
Defy that which has tried to killed us
Daily

But this teacher
Who is breathing heavily on the other end of the phone
Does not care to know this

I am taking up too much time
There are others
On her list to call
Others
With untamed
Young ones
Whose faces she can place
But their names
Escape her
If she has not jotted them on scraps of paper

Careless

We are careless

For allowing her
To forget us

We are careless
For not speaking our names aloud
Declaring
Our presence

Should
Be
Placed in her mouth

We should
Make her speak our names

Teach/her
Our lives are too large

To be documented
On
Scraps of paper

Manhattan Love Song

The dead come back to me, she declares
Of course
She, in her customary careless manner, is referring to
lovers who
For one reason or another have
Come, gone and now returned
To fall into her endless
Ebony
She moves constantly

Wary
Of growing into someone or having them in turn
Take root in her

The dead come back
Seeking warmth
Or rest
Or love

Perhaps they seek retribution
And find them selves
Gathered into the reckless
Net
Of a greedy girl
Who for one reason or another
Allows them
To renter
And defiantly take root

Riot

I will not shut the fuck up
Because
I don't have to

Anymore

I will not shut the fuck up
Because

If I do
Then there is someone or at least a whole lot of
Someone's
Who may fail
To hear

Something is wrong

With
The way
We
Are loving
Breathing
Taking
Stealing
Running
Laying

Still

We are too still

If I am silent
Then this stillness
Will eventually
Stagnate
And I don't want
To die
I don't want
Us to die
I want us

Beautiful
Alive
Loud
Too loud
And
Defiant
But
I want us
Too angry
For stillness
Too angry for silence

And stagnation

I wont **SHUT THE FUCK UP**
I don't have to anymore

I want to speak and listen

Listen to change
Clanking in
The world
Like
Change in pockets of
Undiscovered
Places
Where sunlight
Is unfairly filtered
Shading wrongness
And breeding numbness
Breeding dumbness

Listen I wont **SHUT THE FUCK UP**

And neither should you
Unless the truth is
You have forgotten the sound
Of your own
anger

Poetic Reincarnation

There is blood on this page
Screaming
Ostensible meaning
Into lifeless words

Picture me damaged
Irretrievably
Lost

But still
Spilling myself
Into poems

Defying my own life
Script
Rewriting my death

Awakening in
Verbs
Nouns
Adjectives

I have afterlife
Memories of Sonia Sanchez singing me a lullaby
And Nikki Giovanni writing me whole
again

I am beautifully folded into endless forests
And held delicately in the lips of the ocean
Where I am given
In endless
Kisses to the
Love-struck shore

Anthem to the Superhero Superfreaks

These brothers who live unscripted lives
Excite me
Those men who fly by the seat
Of their baggy pants
Exposing ass cracks for days
Mesmerize me

These brothers are demonized **super hero-super freaks**
They ain't got no damn plan and
Have no idea
Where the next
Day will take them
Instead these
Men/boys
Gather what is right there in front of them
And only believe what they can hold in their hands
To them
Real is obvious
It is tangible - You can pull at it with your teeth or fill your belly with its solidness
What is real is never in question
The only thing to be questioned is the motherfucker that ain't real

I am beautiful to these men
Cause I am
Right here
Larger than life
Falling into their schemes
And believing in their magic
They love my fullness
Softness
Womaness
And they tell me in voices hoarse with
Hustle
How a woman like me is so hard to find
But even harder to keep

My father was one of these men
Always inventing new shit
And dismantling useless shit
Not staying long enough
Or perhaps overstaying his welcome in unfortunate
places
These men
Are in my blood
Damning me with their persistence
And pretty smiles

They walk pretty and smell pretty

And lie lovely

I love these brothers who live unscripted lives
I love them easy, willingly – persistently.
I love them like they are my first drink of water
or my last breath of air
I love these brothers who fly by the seat of their pants
Showing ass crack for days
Leaving mesmerized
Women like
Me
Trembling in
Their wake
with nothing more than memories of their realness
to sustain
us

Life in abstract...

Work.poetrrrry.love.work.child.maaan.
Some mornings I awake
To make
Breakfast for my man
Always hot cereal
With cold milk
My daughter
Always rises way too early before it's even time
To get started
I guess she is too young to not be enamored with life
Sleep, for her, is a necessary evil, but still
It separates her from living
And so she rises too early for me
But just in time for living
I always rise with him
Though
realistically I have until 10 minutes before sunrise to
Shake free dreams and step into the
Tangible
Work.child.work.poetrrry.work.child.maaan.dreams.
breakfastssss.
Some evenings
I try to write
Away
Tend to the needs
Of them folks I call family
And then I find time
To day dream
I throw myself
Down
A surreal
Wishing well
I am a bronzed
Coin
Ffreee falling
And landing heads up
Maybe I will be found
Only to swim in the pockets
Of my captor
Only then to be tossed carelessly,
Forgetfully into a jar

Filled with my
Silver and bronzed
Cousins
This is my family reunion
Us all together
Making
Change
In a see through universe

**Work.work.dreams.child.maaan.me.Ffreedom.
Poetrrrry.**

Acknowledgements

I should first begin by thanking everyone who refused me – those who made me aware of the impossible. These folks taught me what it means to be human. I thank you all because through the lessons bitterly, painfully served by you I found my voice or rather I found cause to open my mouth and scream and out fell words that blossomed into verse. Those verses landed on these pages – hopefully into the hands of folks who will appreciate what I am trying to say.

My most sincerest thanks goes to my nephew, Taheem Jamaal Wells – the original poet. I want to thank you for loving me and inspiring me just by being....your voice is beautifully human.

I have been inspired by the work of so many, most notably, Saul Williams, Jill Scott, Regie Gibson, Sonia Sanchez, Nikki Giovanni, Langston Hughes – I think the collective breaths of these poets litter the air with beauty and I have been blessed to inhale what they exhale.

I want to thank the crowds at the Lizard Lounge, Cantab and the Middle East – thank you for being real and expressing what you like or don't like. Though, I continue to believe the true test of a poem is how it lives on the page, not in the mouth of author, I have absorbed every ounce of your energy and used it to move forward. A special Thank You to Jeff Robinson – Lizard Lounge King – thank you for listening and offering a sistah a poetic home.

Thanks to Trebor Carey, Matt Gallant, the students at Timeberlane Regional High School.and the Café on the Corner in Dover, NH.

To anyone I may have forgotten – you are not forgotten. You exist on these pages, resonating eloquently in rhyme and repetition.

4782017R0

Made in the USA
Charleston, SC
16 March 2010